FAMILY FUN

- Be a weather watcher. Help your child
  draw several pictures of a cloud, the
  sun, and a raindrop on cardboard and
  cut them out. Observe the weather.
  Each day have your child pin the
  appropriate picture to that date on
  a large calendar.

- Measure the rainfall. Place a wide-
  mouthed jar in your yard or on a bal-
  cony. After a rainfall, you and your
  child measure the amount of rain in
  the jar.

- Place a thermometer outside your
  kitchen window. Read the temperature
  with your child each day.

READ MORE ABOUT IT

- *What Is a Cloud?*
- *What Is Thunder and Lightning?*

This book is a presentation of Weekly Reader
Books. Weekly Reader Books offers book
clubs for children from preschool through high
school. For further information write to:
WEEKLY READER BOOKS, 4343 Equity Drive,
Columbus, Ohio 43228

This edition is published by arrangement
with Checkerboard Press.

Weekly Reader is a federally registered trademark
of Field Publications.

WEEKLY READER BOOKS presents

Why Does It Rain?

A **Just Ask**™ Book

by Chris Arvetis

illustrated by
James Buckley

FIELD PUBLICATIONS
MIDDLETOWN, CT.

Look!
It's raining.

It's raining
all around.
Look at the big
raindrops.

Why does it rain?
I've got to find out.

That's a big
question, but
I'll tell you
what I know.

Look around you.
See all the water.
See the lakes, streams,
and puddles.

As the water
is heated,
it turns into
WATER VAPOR.

You can't see
the water vapor,
but it is in the air.
It goes up
into the sky.

The puddle
is smaller!

I know it's hard.
You can't see it happen.
Think of it this way:
The sun heats the water
in the puddles.
Some of the water
soaks into the ground.
Some of the water
evaporates, or goes
up into the air.

I'll take him for a ride.

Let me tell you.
I'll take you into
the sky to show you
what happens next.

As we go up,
the air gets
cooler and
cooler.

That's what happens to the water vapor. As it goes up, it gets cooler and cooler.

Looks like rain!

No doubt!

As the water vapor cools, it forms teeny, tiny drops of water.

When there are
a lot of these
tiny drops of water,
a cloud is formed.

As the air cools more, the tiny drops in the cloud stick together.

The drops get
bigger and heavier.
When they get too big
and heavy, they fall
to the ground.
Hey, wait for me!

Let's
get out
of here!

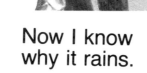